CW01192236

4/6

Dedicated to
Rachel Walker,
granddaughter of
Lady Mary Wentworth-Fitzwilliam.

LADY MARY'S JOURNAL

A VICTORIAN LADY ON HOLIDAY IN ROBIN HOOD'S BAY
13 JULY - 3 AUGUST 1895

Presented by
Patricia Labistour
and Mary Patrick Neads

MARINE ARTS PUBLICATIONS

Copyright © Patricia Labistour and Mary Patrick Neads
All Rights Reserved

Except for use in a review, no part of this publication may be reproduced, stored in a retrieval system, or transmitted in any form or by any means, without prior permission of the publisher.

First published 1997 by Marine Arts Publications
"Seascape"
Robin Hood's Bay,
Whitby, North Yorkshire,
England. YO22 4SH

Flat-Bed Scanning of original Journal by Tim and Ted Cavill of Spectrum Copiers Ltd. 1 Trinity Street, Derringham Street, Hull. HU3 1JR.

Printing and Reprographics by Image Colour Print, Grange Park Lane, Willerby, East Yorks. HU10 6EB.

ISBN 0-9516184-6-6

CONTENTS

INTRODUCTION - by Patricia Labistour

PREFACE - by Mary Patrick Neads

LADY MARY WENTWORTH-FITZWILLIAM'S JOURNAL

An early view of Robin Hood's Bay, prior to the building of the Mount Pleasant area (which grew up around 1885) where Lady Mary stayed. The Victoria Hotel (built 1897) was not there in her day, either.

Note also the Manor House standing in splendid isolation at the Bank Top, and the washing pegged out to dry on the beach.

Lady Mary Wentworth-Fitzwilliam (centre) with Elsie (standing left) and Mab (seated centre). Seated right is 'Aunt Eugene', a friend, Miss Loudon.

INTRODUCTION

Lady Mary Wentworth-Fitzwilliam's Journal is the holiday diary of a titled lady who 'took rooms' in Robin Hood's Bay for three weeks in the summer of 1895.

The coming of the railway to Robin Hood's Bay in 1885 opened up the village to a new economy - that of the 'tourist industry', and many of the large new houses, especially in the Mount Pleasant area, offered accommodation, either with or without 'attendance'. The Fitzwilliams stayed at 'Aldersyde' on Mount Pleasant South.

This diary is a unique record of one of these early holidays, and a real social document of the times.

Lady Mary arrives by train with her two daughters Mab and Elsie, 'Spittles' the lady's maid, Keinz the dachshund, and 'Blobhead Pinbody' Elsie's pet canary. Throughout the holiday, contact is maintained with the family home, Wiganthorpe Hall, near Malton (demolished in 1953) from where necessary 'supplies' are regularly obtained to help assist their accustomed standard of living.

Mab (Marie Albreda Blanche) and Elsie (Isabel Elizabeth Mary) were 17 and 15 years old at the time - still young enough to enjoy the pleasures of the beach and plenty of good food!

Lady Mary had a *penchant* for nicknames: Elsie is referred to in the journal as 'the Pelse' (for some unexplained reason), the girls jointly as 'the Girshas', and Lady Mary herself as 'Mim' or 'Mimsie' - often with a somewhat confusing rapid change of tense!

The original handwritten text has been faithfully transcribed by Mary Patrick Neads, and transferred into a more readable typestyle by Patricia Labistour, and all Lady Mary's miniature watercolours have been included as they appear in her journal. Additional contemporary watercolours of 'Bay, believed to have been painted by a daughter of the Rev. Jermyn Cooper in 1893, and some by Patricia Labistour 'in the style of Lady Mary' have been included to further enhance the text. The photographs are believed to have been taken by Ulric Walmsley* at the direction of Lady Mary, as described in the journal, and published here for the first time. A recently re-published postcard from a glass slide shows an aristocratic lady visitor by the boats. It would have been nice to assume that this may have been Lady Mary herself, but her granddaughter is certain that it is not. This postcard is reproduced by kind permission of Mr Peter Cooper who currently owns the original glass slide, very possibly an Ulric Walmsley acquired when Ulric's wife, Jane, had a 'clearing out' and gave some items to Peter's mother. As Lady Mary had been specific in directing Ulric towards certain views, we consider it highly likely that she *could* have posed for her own picture!

Especial thanks are extended to Miss Rachel Walker, daughter of Mab, and granddaughter of Lady Mary, who has kindly given her blessing to this project, and to whom, therefore, this book is dedicated.

---

*Ulric Walmsley was a well known artist and father of the author Leo Walmsley. He brought his family to live in Robin Hood's Bay in 1894, the year before the writing of the holiday diary. Their house in King Street is marked with a blue plaque.

PREFACE

You may wonder how such a gem of a journal could lie dormant for over a hundred years but it was a matter of the opportunity being presented at the right time.

It so happened that in the summer of 1895 Lady Mary Wentworth Fitzwilliam of Wiganthorpe Hall, near Malton in the North Riding of Yorkshire took her two young daughters, Mab and Elsie, for a three week holiday to Robin Hood's Bay, near Whitby.

Lady Mary records their visit in a red Moroccan leather exercise book with gilt edges for which she paid 4/6 and this has never been rubbed out. Not only was she a competent writer of daily happenings but she illustrated their holiday with charming little paintings. Like all good things their visit came to an end and the journal was completed except for one or two blank spaces which had been reserved for further paintings but alas, they were never done. However, these spaces have been adequately filled.

Thirty-four years later, Lady Mary died, and her journal passed into the hands of her younger daughter, Miss Elsie Fitzwilliam, for by now they had come to live at Slingsby Hall, near Malton.........

............and now to tell you how the journal slowly came to life again.

Meanwhile, my parents, the Rev. Arthur and Mrs. Patrick who lived at Robin Hood's Bay Vicarage for six years, left to take up the parish of Slingsby in 1949. This is when we met Miss Elsie Fitzwilliam.

To all, Miss Elsie was a most friendly woman and helpful to everyone. She was a great animal lover and in her younger days she had been a leading judge at Siamese Cat Shows. In her retirement she shared her home with many feline friends. Then there was Piggy. Yes, it was a real pig who followed Miss Elsie about like a dog.

It was on a summer's day when the meadows were bright with buttercups and the gardens ablaze with flowers that Miss Elsie walked up the lane to our house with Piggy, carrying a brown paper parcel in her hand. The parcel was given to my mother. When she opened it she found inside a unique record of a holiday at Robin Hood's Bay written fifty-five years ago.

Who better would appreciate this than someone who had lived at Robin Hood's Bay and had loved the village? Coupled to that was the fact Lady Mary had also lived in Slingsby........it seemed a happy coincidence.

From this point the diary started its journey back to life when, following the death of my mother it came into my hands.

One day whilst browsing through my book case I picked up the journal and began to read it. At first I found the writing difficult to follow for there was also a scattering of foreign words together with 'made up words' known only to the family. However, I became more and more absorbed and decided the only way to appreciate the journal to the full was to transcribe it. Then I would be able to read it in its entirety without having to puzzle over words.

By the time I had finished my task I realized that I had uncovered a gem of past history and also a work written with such unassuming simplicity that one has a sense of trespass in reading it.

Several years later I met Patricia Labistour of Robin Hood's Bay. A woman with a sensitive feeling for her village, she, I was sure, would be most interested to read the journal accompanied by the transcript. At this stage there was no particular thought of publishing, but about two weeks later when I visited Patricia to collect my precious property it was obvious that she too had thoroughly enjoyed reading it and had found it fascinating. We started to discuss the possibility of publishing the journal and so after 102 years it began to stir into life with Pat in charge of the presentation and drawings.

The next step was for me to find Lady Mary's immediate relatives. At Old Malton I found to my delight that Mab had married Major Harold Maxwell Walker and became the mother of two daughters. One of them survived and I was able to contact Miss Rachel Walker, granddaughter of Lady Mary, who has been most helpful and patient with my enquiries and to whom we are indebted.

But what about the author, Lady Mary Wentworth-Fitzwilliam? Certainly she was a very talented and clever woman. She was born in 1846, the daughter of the Second Marquis of Ormonde at Kilkenny Castle in Ireland, and was christened Mary Grace Louisa. The family name was Butler.

Her journal shows that Lady Mary was intensely interested in all around her. Her love of animals and her interest in people were paramount. Lady Mary was a linguist, speaking fluent French, German and Italian, and she could read Russian, no mean achievement. Certainly this must have been a great asset to her when she was appointed Lady-in-Waiting to the Duchess of Edinburgh (Marie, daughter of Alexander II, Tsar of Russia) who had married Queen Victoria's second son, Prince Alfred. The appointment was made about 1870 and lasted until Lady Mary's own marriage in 1877 to William Henry Wentworth-Fitzwilliam. But the friendship with the Duchess lasted a lifetime and occasionally Lady Mary was recalled to be an Extra Lady-in-Waiting.

She was also a diligent reader of the Bible. Her own copy is full of passages which she has underlined and comments fill the margins.

Lady Mary's marriage was a long and happy one which ended on July 10th 1920 with the death of her husband.

On that day she poignantly and bravely wrote the following in her Bible:-

"And now I must strive to do what remains to be done unguided by the voice which as long as I could appeal to it never failed me.
July 10th 1920"

The next year Wiganthorpe Estate was sold and Lady Mary with Miss Elsie Fitzwilliam temporarily moved to Bransby.

   However, in 1925 Slingsby Hall became available which Lady Mary bought. By now she was an old woman, and in poor health. On January 17th 1929 Lady Mary died peacefully and was buried with her husband at Wentworth, the seat of the Fitzwilliam family.

   And so ended an interesting life beginning in the reign of Queen Victoria when horsepower gave way to mechanization. Then came the terrible slaughter of the 1914-18 war and twenty years later the rumbles of another war began to be felt. Meanwhile, new inventions were being made daily; never before had the tempo of life quickened so dramatically.

   Times have changed greatly since Lady Mary's day, but I hope you will enjoy this singular glimpse of the past.

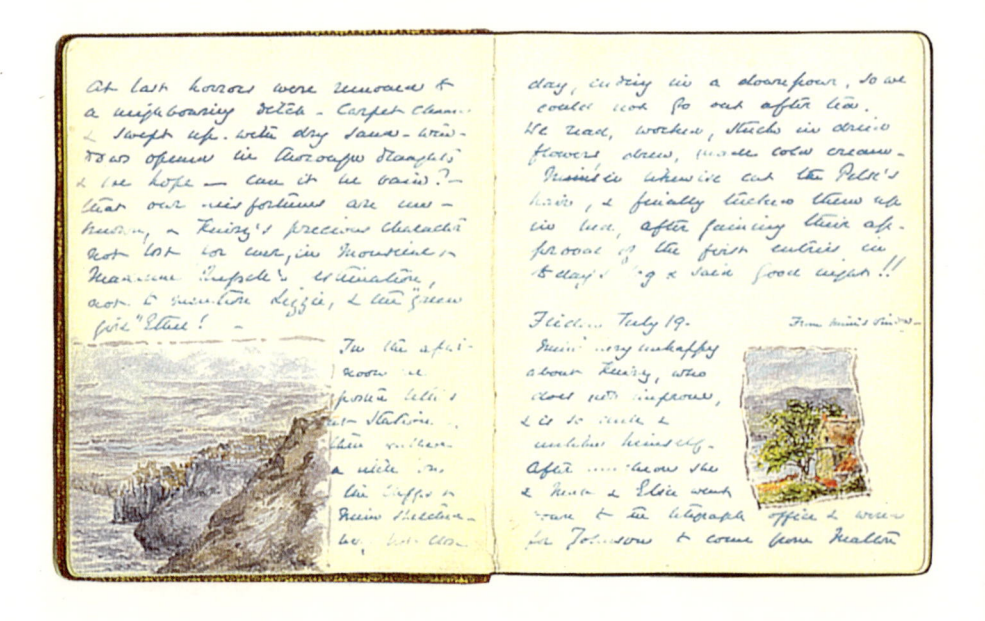

Lady Mary in later life.

Mabsew & Elsie
from Mimsie

Robin Hood's Bay
1895

Saturday July 13th 1895

    We, that is Mab, Elsie and Mim, accompanied by Spittles, Keinz the Dachs, Mim's Tishia and Elsie's canary left Wigganthorpe soon after luncheon en route for Robin Hood's Bay and the sea. Long wait at Malton, spent principally in munching cherries and buying honey, longer wait at Whitby where we missed the 4.21 p.m. train. We thought the line very pretty indeed and it was a lovely day. Mab related that the Station Master's wife at Hovingham used to come to Whitby for a little change, but that she shrieked so at each bend of the line which goes like this *Malton*〰〰〰 *Whitby* that the Station Master gave up going there.

We walked down the pier and watched the waves, there was a big sea on. We bought buns and ate them in a shop, they were yellow with "fruit" in a heap in a corner of them and besmeared with sugar on top, but we found them good.

At 6.35 p.m. we started again and got to Robin Hood's Bay shortly after 7.p.m. Mim had been greatly exercised in mind over an artist and his work they had seen in Whitby who she admired. She tried to explain to the bairns that a sketch may be more like which gives you the impression of what you see, than one which draws every line of the nearest house in the foreground but the girls failed to be convinced.

We were very glad of our tea and when we had helped Spittles to unpack and had settled up our rooms comfortably, we started off for the sea, though it was nearly 9.p.m. It is an extraordinary place this Robin Hood's Bay. The little town is built anyhow, up a steep cliff from the actual shore - narrow streets, often nothing but shallow steps, high houses, strange passages, a deep gully running through the town with masses of convolvulus hanging in great festoons down its sides and houses perched looking sheer down to the bottom of the gully.

The Bolts.

The information that Robin Hood's Bay was formerly a stronghold for smugglers seemed so absolutely in harmony with its whole appearance that it seemed only quite right and natural that it should be so, such a pity if it weren't.

Anything more picturesque cannot be imagined, and here and there a narrow passage seen through an arch or under

The Bolts from the Main Street. One of the 'Bay's smuggling escape routes - named from the fact that men escaping from the Preventives or Press Gang, could conveniently 'bolt' into the nearby densely wooded countryside.

a wooden gallery or bridge, an opening into a small court overhung with greenery of sorts is very Italian and most surprizing to find high up in Yorkshire. The tide was in, and little beach in consequence, the night warm and still.

    The one or two lamps the little town boasts were lighted as we returned home, and the effects of the light and shade from them and open doors and lighted windows in the narrow, dark, tortuous streets were very weird and attractive. We were all glad to go to bed but the impression of our little sea view "Aufenthalt" [place of abode - residence] is distinctly a pleasant one.

Sunday July 14th

A lovely morning, were not ready for early church, settled to go in the evening. Read together the Morning Service.

The name of our marine residence is 'Aldersyde' the landlord and landlady

'Aldersyde', Mount Pleasant South.

are Mr. and Mrs. Emmerson Russell - he is a builder. She suffers from heart complaint - both nice people. We are "done for" in a very primitive fashion by Mrs. Russell's friend Lizzie, assisted by a "green fire" as they say in Ireland. All very amiable and doing their best to make us happy. It is expected that Spittles takes her meals with us, except when specially invited to tea with our "patrons". The arrangement suits us perfectly. We have a drawing room, a dining room, a double bedded room (2 beds) for Mab and Elsie, Mim's room looking on to the sea and Spittles' room, a narrow apartment next to it.

We glory however in a hot and cold bathroom and everything so simple to a degree, is very clean and we are very satisfied - only the butter!! that is ferociously evil, with thankfulness we bless the happy idea of buying honey at Malton. Mr. Harris, the dentist told me a friend of his, a doctor, besides boiling water and milk for fear of infection, likewise boiled the butter. No amount of boiling would un-taste this butter, of that I am sure.

Walked in the afternoon. Church at 6.30 sat in pews with ill conditioned boys who had supplied themselves with a hearty meal of raw peas in the shell with which they diverted themselves the whole time, assisting their digestion with an animated conversation carried on in whispers till the service ended.

We began "To Right the Wrong" by Edna Lyall in the evening.

Monday July 15th

Mim sat up early in bed and sketched view from window - arrives Elsie asking unnecessary questions as to which skirt she and Mab would put on, what colour shirt etc. Mim preoccupied answers vaguely. Elsie descants to Mab at length on the hopelessness of her case, "as Mim is only thinking of her drawing". Went to Whitby by 1.3.p.m. train after early luncheon to buy jerseys, Tam-o-Shanters etc to face the tremendous wind here, which wriggles the feathers off our hats and the hair off our heads. Lovely day but wind awful - after the outfitters, proceeded to St. Hilda's Abbey which really is very fine indeed and we bought a small book in a pale green cover for the sum of 1 penny to inform our minds withall on the subject.

Did other small shoppings including more honey and a tin of biscuits for the hungry bairns at odd moments. They are Carr's American Crackers price 2/- the tin.

We bought soap, we bought "Mearcurion" for sixpence, we bought glue and blue ink. We had coffee and buns at our old haunt and were just late for the 4.21 train but the good station master whistled it back for us and we got back about 5.p.m. Finished "Kidnapped" in evening.

'Peak' Ravenscar

Robin Hood's Town from the South. 'Beacholme' was once a ship builders - note the half-completed coble on what is now The Quarterdeck.

Tuesday July 16th

Raining and very wild. Long afternoon on shore, girls hunting for shrimps of which they caught a good dish full getting excessively wet. Mim who caught four sea anemones and curiosities for our aquarium we propose to start, also noting picturesque "bits" fit to sketch on a finer day. Back for 6.pm tea. Weather damp and much colder - thankful for a little fire in evening. Capital accounts in papers of 'Unionist' successes. Arrival of fresh butter, fruit and flowers from Wigganthorpe. Mim, Mab and Elsie, a huge dish of strawberries disappearing rapidly between them. Mab, "Mimsie, Elsie is stuffing such a lot of strawberries, she'll soon burst". Elsie, "Certainly I am getting quite fulfilled, but I mean to stop short of bursting."

Keinz is poorly. Mim not happy about him - he gorges on foulnesses on the beach, old habit, skate remains etc, the smell of which reaches us already from afar. He is recommended a dose of finely powdered glass for 3 mornings and then some castor oil and olive oil mixed. Mab and Elsie greatly enjoy administering these potions.

<u>Wednesday July 17th</u>

Saw in York Herald that Milton is returned for Wakefield, wrote to congratulate. Rained hard in the morning, less wind - cleared about midday, but still appeared threatening. Got into our new jersies and Tam o' Shanters and defied all weathers. Elsie finds her shoes too tight, says she "now possesses two skins, the new one considerably tighter than the old."

We walked to Thorpe after luncheon and then to the church and old churchyard above. So many "lost at sea" "drowned" "lost from upsetting of Life Boat" or "collision at sea" most pathetic of all "in memory of those who never returned" "missing" "sailed on such a day and not heard of again" or "supposed to have gone down with all hands".

Old St. Stephen's Church.

A few funny old epitaphs are:
"I have a tender father been
And troubles sore my life has seen,
In everything I did my best
And now my body is at rest"

After tea we went for a long walk on the beach. Mab and Elsie collecting many stones and shells for future use and for Mim's benefit. We bought lime juice medicaments for the Keinz in a curious little chemist shop at the top of the gulley. Got coffee ground for us at the grocers, a brother of our landlord, also photographs of Whitby and this place. Evening spent arranging treasures, boiling out the shell fish and nursing the beautiful Brown, who is exceedingly limp. Sea air doesn't suit the Keinz.

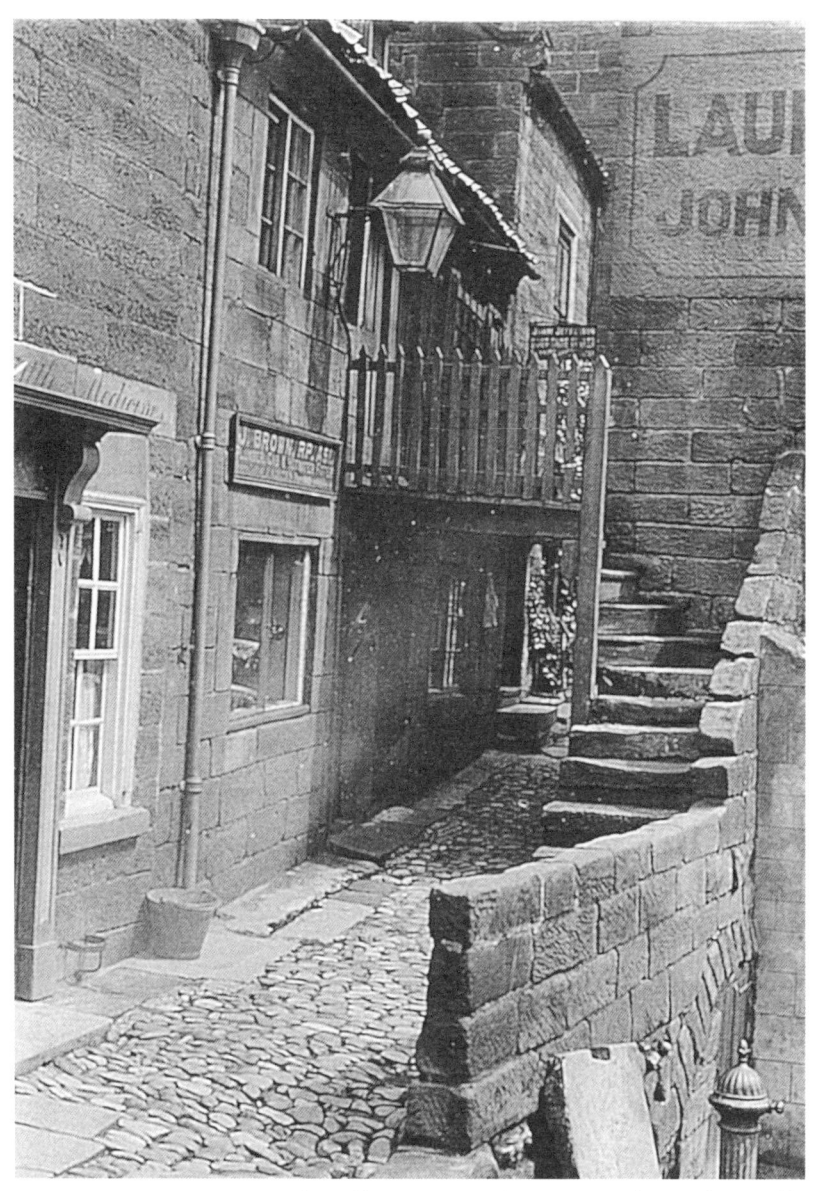

Martin's Row - next to the Old Forge was the Farrier's shop, which sold Cattle Medicines. This was where Lady Mary bought the strange medicaments for The Keinz.

Thursday July 18th

First thing in the morning Mab and Elsie arrived *chez Mimmsie* to administer a dose of castor oil and olive oil mixed to my poor Brown -

Second thing was *meine Herr von Keinz* retired under Mim's bed and was sick.

Thirdly, Mab and Elsie employed themselves usefully by sanding and removing horrors, for which Mim owes them miles of gratitude.

Fourthly, Keinz was sick again in front of Mim's dressing table while Mim was in the bathroom.

Fifthly, Mab and Elsie renewed their charitable task.

Sixthly, we discovered that *Mein Herr* was in the daily habit of frequenting the pig pail, the dust heap and eating the other dog's dinner, besides regaling himself on old habit and savoury garbage on the seaboard!!

Seventhly, Mim issued stern words for the future and my beautiful Brown was conducted to walk on his chain today.

Eighthly, while we were at tea, Mab and Elsie just starting on some tasty cutlets, Mim pre-occupied with bread and honey - ominous sounds from Keinz's basket filled our souls with alarm.

Mab leading the forlorn hope made a rush to his basket to seize him and carry him captive to the open air alas! Too late for the third time today the awful catastrophe was re-enacted - poor us and miserable Brown!! He however curled himself up in his red blankets to sleep the sleep of the relieved just - we had to rush for sand, scrapers, beesoms. Mim all but following Keinz's example, leant against the door on guard to prevent witnesses from approaching and feeling pea green within and without, for the Girshas said "Poor Mim, and she does love her sweet scents so much." Mim could only faintly applaud the heroism of her bairns for speaking at all was difficult. At last horrors were removed to a neighbouring ditch, carpet cleaned and swept with dry sand - windows opened in thorough draughts and we hope - can it be vain that our misfortunes are unknown and Keinz's precious character not lost forever in Monsieur and Madame Russell's estimation, not to mention Lizzie and the "Green Fire Ethel"!

    In the afternoon we posted letters at the Station and then walked a little on the cliffs and Mim sketched, very hot close day ending in a down pour so we could not go out after tea. We read, worked, stuck in dried flowers, drew, made cold cream.

    Mimsie likewise cut the Pelse's hair, and finally tucked them up in bed, after gaining their approval of the first entries in to-day's log and said Good-night!

<u>Friday July 19th</u>

    Mim's very unhappy about Keinz who does not improve and is so dull and unlike himself. After luncheon, she, Mab and Elsie went down to the telegraph office and wired for Johnson to come from Malton to see him and advise. Except to send the telegram Mim did not leave the Brown all day and he seemed happier with her near him. Got some Bovril and fed him every hour as he absolutely refuses food of any sort and takes no interest in anything but seems to sleep all day.

From Mim's window.

    Mab and Elsie went out with Spittles to Thorpe in the morning and on the beach in the afternoon. About 8-15 pm Johnson arrived to inspect my Brown who has got worms very badly indeed, aggravated by all the shore garbage he has indulged in, the darling. He hopes he will pull round alright but must take him away and thoroughly look after him and dose him. He is very weak he says, and the Bovril was quite right. After a dose of Chlorodyne Keinz seemed brighter but he is so awfully limp and miserable.

Mim passed most of the day beside him, making small sketches when possible. The likeness - bar colouring - and some bits of Robin Hood's Bay town and some at Venice is always striking Mim and she harangues the Girshas to that effect and draws examples to prove her point.

Venice.

There being no late train here, Johnson has a room for the night and carried off *das Keinzerli* at an early hour this morning.

<u>Saturday July 20th</u>

Mim got up betimes to see her beautiful Brown before he left in his basket with his two scarlet blankets - carried basket and all under Johnson's arm. The Keinz looked up remonstrating at her desertion of him and Mim watched him out of sight from her window.

A very rainy day, thick mist over the sea, a perfect curtain of grey over the land.

Mab and Elsie distinctly above themselves - obstreperous and Mim truly thankful when the heavy rain ceasing they were able, all 3 to get into jerseys and shortest of skirts and go off for a long walk. Went through Thorpe to the hill beyond (Sledgates) above the clouds as Elsie remarked when we emerged from the rain we had endured there, and, looking back saw the mist lying thick on the hill top. But far out over the Bay it looked clearer, the clouds seemed rolling up higher with bright edges below, and leaving pale blue glimpses of sky between them and we prophesied a fine evening after all. The beloved sea has been very smooth all day, very grey, scarcely a white fringe where the waves break on the beach.

Robin Hood's Bay Railway Station.

We posted letters at the Station office and watched the trains coming in from Scarboro' and Whitby, got back about 5.30 and tea time, somewhat damp and the Girshas excessively concerned to wring the wet out of their red caps assuring me that the rain had been dripping on their heads, that they felt it, the inside of their caps being perfectly dry. Mim failed to express the least sympathy, especially as wearing one herself, she had experienced not one of the singular sensations. The Keinz's absence and things weighed much on Mim's mind and she does not quite realise he is away. The bairns laugh when now and then from habit she looked round for him or expects him - the little horrors!!

We are having a fire lighted which refuses to burn. Mademoiselle Lizzie is *á genoux [on her knees]* before it, striking matches and rustling paper, but with no visible effect. Meanwhile the evening is getting lovely but after our wetting we must bide at home and get our clothes dry. Flowers, butter, etc arrive from Wigganthorpe and the Girshas have "surprized" me with lovely arrangements of roses, such a smart room for Sunday. I am keen to go to the Congregational Chapel where all the sailors go to-morrow evening - think it would be nice.

Congregational Chapel, Fisherhead.

Sunday July 21st

Letters did not arrive until after church, found them on my return from service - very wet afternoon. The Girshas more or less dèsoeuerée [idle, not wanting to work]. Things marched fairly well as long as stern Mim kept up the discipline and found employment for idle hands and still idler brains but after tea Mim went to the Wesleyan Chapel and as neither bairn showed much zeal for a second church going, she left them behind. On her return, though it was pouring with rain, both Girshas rushed down the terrace, bareheaded to meet her, because Elsie said, now dull care could be gone. As far as Mim makes out, they spent the whole time of her absence jawing. The little simple service

Chapel Street, Robin Hood's Bay.

at the Wesleyan chapel was very pleasant and earnest, besides being the anniversary of the Infant Sunday School being established. The old lady next whom Mim sat after the service was over, proudly presented the Preacher to her, "my nephew".

Wesleyan Chapel, Chapel Street.

Monday July 22nd

Lovely morning, Mim anxiously awaiting the post and news of Keinz. That he is "rather less sick and rather better too" is a great relief. We went early to the shore as it is now high tide in the afternoon. We bought a pail for plunder at *Mein Herr* Moorsom's warehouse on the way down price 3d. Elsie shrimped and caught a nice little bowl full.

Mim sketched the neighbouring 'head' Fisherhead. Mab read to her. A hot bright sun, delicious air but heavy clouds about. Bought some shady hats for the shore 3d. each. On the way up seeing a photographer busy at work taking views, Mim extremely officiously found it incumbent on her how to teach him how to do his own business. She entered into friendly conversation with him, instructing him as to where she considered he and the other local photographers failed -

corrected him, apparatus and all to what she considered characteristic of Robin Hood's Bay, helped him to fix the exact site - gave him no end of a trouble, smirked when he acknowledged her artistic powers, by no means modestly denied them, but found him perfectly right in saying what he did, patronizingly assured him she should come and see the result of their united labours and graciously accepting his thanks for all the trouble she had given him - made her farewells and *au revoirs* and carried the Girshas off to luncheon, feeling she had nobly forwarded the cause of art and science.

Rain again in afternoon - hoped to get out after tea, which we ordered earlier in consequence, but no such luck. The girls rejoiced in Shrimps and Lobsters for tea - Much smashing of claws on carpets - Mim remonstrating and insisting on sweepings up of remnants. Also of washing most unsavoury fingers after tea.

    Writing up log - pressing and sticking in of dried flowers - reading etc whiles away the rainy season. Yesterday evening Mim had occasion to call Mab "Baby Bunting". Elsie immediately proposes to dress her in a rabbit skin, nothing else. Mim "How shall we make it fit? How shall we put her into it, head first or feet?" Elsie, "Feet first and bend her knees backwards so that the rabbit's skin shouldn't go wrong." Mim, "I'm not sure she'll look very nice in it anyways." Elsie, "Not long, for I'll get into a fox's skin and eat her up."

Tuesday July 23rd

    Saw in papers first thing this morning that Mr. Fison is in for Doncaster - went off to the town and telegraphed congratulations to him.

    Wandered about Robin Hood's Bay, conversed with an old sailor who afterwards took us to his house where we saw some nice birds his son, who is buried seven weeks ago had brought home.

    Then he took us to see his daughter and another beautiful green parrot with a blue patch on his head. She took us all over her house, a good type of these Robin Hood's Bay erections - very high - quite beautifully clean, two or even three entrances on different levels and passages, handy for smugglers, narrow winding stairs and narrowest of lanes between the houses - funny little gardens or bits of greenery turning up in unexpected places, all extremely well kept - the rooms having a decided impression of ships cabins. We were shown everything, and Mim as usual investigated all the family history with great interest - saw also all the family photographs and the family album - family in the house consisting of 7 own bairns and 5 orphans - children of the poor consumptive brother lately dead. The good woman told me that last Sunday they had sat down 14 to dinner and that her old father and two friends from Sunderland had joined them. They were all poor fisher folk but it was awfully nice being with them.

    Mim and the girls were shown the bed where the brother had died and then the old sailor's father offered to take them to see his cousin, who had a picture of a whaler stuck in the ice. Mim at once accepted and soon we were on our way in and out of these extraordinary passages, steep steps and windings and turnings.

Then we arrived at a most picturesque spot, up steps, white roses growing over green palings, houses one on top of the other as usual and were shown into another smartish of little "cabins", houses are polished and shining and ornamented with a cutlass or two, a harpoon with "Valiant" engraved across it and the celebrated picture. The owner of all the glory, a very nice dignified old man - alas! only recently recovered from a paralytic stroke which had affected his speech. This combined with the broadest of Yorkshire made the 8th sense of Intuition extremely necessary but on the whole we got on very well and acquired a good

Martin's Row.

deal of knowledge as to the whale fishery which, however, seems dying out. Our first friend then conducted us by a new passage towards our destination and we said an affectionate "farewell" and "au revoir" and Mim is going to hasten and finish a comforter for him, as a souvenir, he told us he is 82 next week. We visited Mr. Moorsom's emporium and paid a debt of 3 pence. We visited Madame Granger's somewhat fancy warehouse and bought Rob Roy cups and saucers for 6½ d the two. We called on Mim's friend the photographer to see if he had been successful in the views Mim had inculcated - one was already printed for her inspection and is capital. He asked her for more suggestions as he was just off to take some more views - Needless to say, Mim was perfectly ready to do so and told him of one or two advantageous points of view.

We meant to drive to Falling Foss but weather seemed doubtful and the experienced advised us to wait so we deferred our pony and trap to another day.

In the afternoon called on Mr. Richardson. Nothing daunted that <u>Mrs</u> Richardson was 'out'. He had been very kind in helping Mr. Hartley to get this booking for us - Such a cheery house with a most perfect view from the many windows and full of really nice carvings à l'ancienne [in an old fashioned style] of his own. Also he had some nice real old bits, the patterns of which Mim covets for work designs. Mim bought a few photographs at Madame Granger's for sticking in. They arrived in a hard parcel and Mim squealed with dismay thinking they had been expressly mounted for her, but to her relief found it was only extra precaution and she expressed the weight off her mind to the Girshas in a most original song!!

"Now Mrs. Granger careful soul,
Had two stout cardboards found,
To pack the photos which she loved
And keep them safe and sound!"

"Oh Mim!" "Oh Mim, you are so funny. What puts these things in your head?" from the two attentive bairns.

We bought some hats price 3d. for the sun today - they will add another feature to our already somewhat desultory style of dress for the seaboard. Spittles despises them from the bottom of her heart. Mais!!

After tea the Pelse and I took a walk on the cliffs south of the town - a most lovely evening, glass going up. Colouring on sea and town perfectly beautiful. Bales from Wigganthorpe - butter, fruit - heard of awful thunderstorm there on Sunday - no wonder it looked so black here.

Elsie reminded me out walking and wished it inserted in the log, that when Mim was discoursing the photographer on the proper way of taking views of Robin Hood's Bay town she remarked to him on one of his photographs taken from the beach at very low tide.

- "This one is the best for me, only I can't understand why you didn't take it when the tide was in, it would be so much more characteristic"!

Mim didn't understand why the poor man's consent was feeble, until enlightened by her daughters on the way home!!

All the same, she isn't sure that Elsie's assurance that Mim's remarks always "amuse her vastly" is quite as seriously reverential as the Mimsie might expect.

One of our great amusements now is watching the coast railway trains mounting the cliffs. The ascent is marvellous.

No fresh news of my beautiful Brown, so Mim trusts no news is good news. She has however sent postcards to Johnson for daily transmission of bulletins.

The area around 'Beacholme' attracted various activities. Notice the sets of wheels awaiting the return of the cobles which would then be drawn up onto the shallow cliffs at this point. Also, the six compartment pigeon loft on the wall.

<u>Wednesday July 24th</u>

A postcard from Johnson telling me that my little Keinz has the jaundice and is seriously ill though in other respects a little better. Am feeling very miserable and anxious about my little dog. Pouring wet morning - clearing in afternoon. Went for a long walk to the funny little village of "Raws". Raw I think it is called, the most disconnected village we ever saw but picturesque as to position and the lovely view of Robin Hood's Bay from it. Returned by Fylingdale and Thorpe. Tea at 5. The bairns edified by mushrooms. After tea prepared and arranged flowers - read "Catriona" and drew.

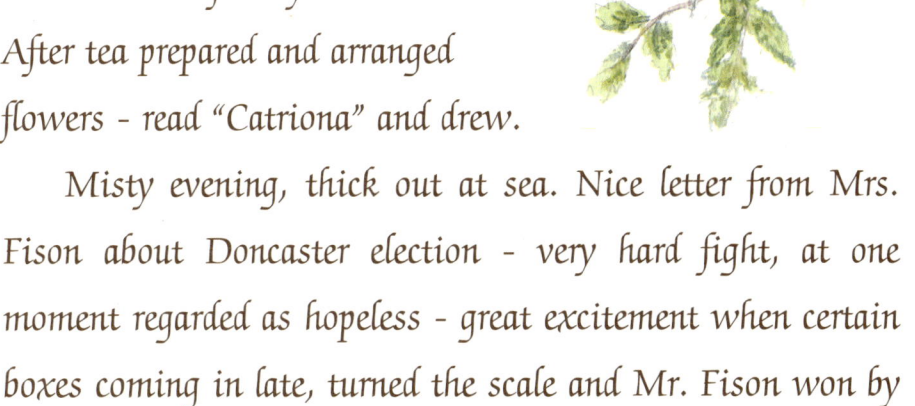

Misty evening, thick out at sea. Nice letter from Mrs. Fison about Doncaster election - very hard fight, at one moment regarded as hopeless - great excitement when certain boxes coming in late, turned the scale and Mr. Fison won by 141 majority. In evening Harry wrote to like effect. At the counting up the miners votes were so overwhelmingly in Mr. Walton's favour that the Unionist despaired - suddenly the tide changed and they all went mad when the poll was declared - Both sides mad, in a way, hoped and doubted during the contest.

The Station Master very kindly finds out and sends me the election news which he gets by telegram. This moment I receive a note from him to say Wharton in for Ripon. 702 majority.

Robin Hood's Bay from the north cliffs.

<u>Thursday July 25th</u>

Rather better account of my dear little Keinz this morning, which makes Mim happier than she was yesterday and a little more hopeful. An awful fog since yesterday evening - the fog horns and whistles heard all through the night.

A dull foggy rainy day - pouring at moment and as thick a fog out at sea as can be imagined, the near coast, let alone Peak Ravenscar being absolutely invisible, really one can only see to the nearest hedge. A long day indoors, for going out in this dripping weather, with so little accommodation for drying clothes etc in the house was impossible. So we managed as well we could. Did our studies in the morning, then needlework and "Catriona" reading out loud alternately, Mim painting the while till her turn came. Also we stuck in our prepared flowers and hunted out their names which Mim wrote in her best handwriting and the Girshas say they can't read it, sorry!!

Later the bairns helped pack a box for return to Wigganthorpe thankful to find something to do - Mim had suggested that they should go and wash their handkerchiefs or shirts as a recreation combining usefulness!!

The conversation was not particularly brilliant or amusing but we often laughed - Mim is a bit throaty and depressed, perhaps in consequence, perhaps about her dear Brown, perhaps because the fog got a wee little inside? Which, my bairns? However we all made the best of everything.

Wartburg.

As we were walking near Raws yesterday we met an old man herding some cows and Mim stopped to converse with him, "Good evening Sir"! he answered "Good evening Miss". Mim said to the girls, "It's distinctly trying being called Miss with you two big girls in tow." Elsie answered, "But you see you give so much more the impression of being "Missy" than "Ma'ammy". For which she had to be chased and Mimmsie realised the peculiar advantage and humility to see ourselves as others see us, especially when it is to the occasion of our bairns.

Elsie dropped an enormous darning needle with which she apparently predicts doing her canvas work. She looked for it with vigour "because (quoting the following refined and expressive lines)

There was a young lady of Cheadle
Who sat down in church on a needle
But though deeply imbedded
It was luckily threaded
And swiftly pulled out by the Beadle!

That might be her case, but you see Mimsie, my needle is not threaded!" 9 p.m. and pouring, pouring, pouring and the fog thicker than ever out at sea. Elsie says the glass is going down but Mab thinks that may here be the sign of fine weather - *Speriano!* *[let's hope so!]*. Mim writes awaiting a squeal from her bairns from above to say they are ready to be tucked in and read to, before curling up and snoring low snores of the just - or unjust maybe!!

A collier brig unloading coal on Robin Hood's Bay beach.

Friday July 26th

Raining heavily this morning and still thick out at sea and the fog horns going but at all counts you could not cut the fog with a knife and preserve a piece as a keepsake of Robin Hood's Bay as one perfectly could yesterday. We resolved, come what may to go out after luncheon regardless of consequences - Mim read "Mareniose" to the Girshas as literature this morning in honour of "high Whitby's cloistered pile". During luncheon it cleared a good bit and out we went in the somewhat desultory costume we affect here but necessarily.

After posting letters at the Station we roamed the cliffs, everything dripping wet, and the ground a perfect soup of slippery mud. The cliffs are breaking away in all directions, many a small landslip did we mark and places where whole bits of wall have disappeared and where railings have had to be put further back. Mim distinctly 'jumpy' when near the edge of a cliff herself, still 'jumpier' when the Girshas shin the outskirts thereof.

Cliff edge cottages from the end of Cliff Street.

We watched the sea-gulls for some time, wheeling in all directions, having nests and young ones there and delighted in their wild cry. We collected flowers to press and found one or two we didn't know and hadn't got.

Then we left the cliff and made inland, trespassed on a cornfield and were warned not to do so again by a remarkably cross man, although there was a path round the whole field to which we religiously kept.

Mim apologised, Mab was haughty and said she should go again whenever she liked - Mim recommended humility and not to put herself in the wrong - Mab assured her she never wanted to go in that field again. Mim thought this remarkably sensible of her under the circumstances.

Tea early that, if fine, we might go out again - but there were sharp showers and it thundered a good deal and heavy clouds coming up and a certain suspicious mistiness about

Peak which we have learned to misdoubt. So we did not dare to go far afield - posted more letters, walked to Thorpe, then round by church.

Watched the train going by the coast line, forgot to look at the most interesting moment when it reaches the Peak and returned to 'Aldersyde', not knowing what else quite to do in face of uncertain clouds and sounds and condition of roads. Mab, moreover, having put on a pair of India rubber boots with a leak on the upperside so the long craggs and morass would ill have suited their constitution.

"What shall we do, Mimsie?"
"Have a game of Halma first and then stick in your flowers and I'll read 'Catriona' to you. Now I'm going to look at 'The Times'."
So the Girshas bickered and squabbled over Halma, each thinking the other played disgustingly and thinking to tell her so in plainest language till

when two games had been fought out to the bitter end of both tongues, Mim called for a truce - the needlework was produced and till bed-time we excited ourselves over the adventures of "Alan Breck and David Balfour", Mim getting so harassed that she had to look on, despite the pipings of her young!!

The reports of my little Keinz were better this morning and Mim's spirits revived in consequence. Thundering in the distance, and flashes of sheet lightning continually.

When tucking up the bairns Mim captured a whole lump of well-kneaded wax under Elsie's pillow, the pastime is to roll it about in her hands. It seemed innocent and Mim's stoney heart relented and she restored the confiscated property for which she got extra warmly embraced by her daughter.

Saturday July 27th

Accounts of my beautiful Brown this morning are very good. "Marked improvement in Keinz, going on satisfactory" and Mim feels much better.

A tremendous thunderstorm in the night and by no means quite cleared off this morning. Went to Thorpe and called and took refuge from the thunderous downpelt in Mr. Richardson's house - only saw him, but left a card on Madame. Enquired, from him, the best way to get to Peak, indulging visions, in case thunderstorms are appeased - of ambling off there this afternoon.

Directly after luncheon, and when the needful amount of gooseberries had been assimilated by Mab and Elsie, likewise figs and peaches by us all, we got into our shortest of skirts, our bluest of jerseys, our caps and sailor hats and the water tightest boots we can collect, determined to brave the ascent. A perfect afternoon, very lovely in colouring, fresh and alive after the storm.

We went down the town and at the bottom, espying some truly beautiful buns in a baker's shop by the post Mim stopped, "Mab, do you think if I asked them to let me have 3 buns without paying for them, they would? I haven't a farthing of money." "I'm sure I don't know", says Mab. "Try", says Elsie. So Mim went in and smiling sweetly on a fair young man with spectacles said, "Will you trust me to pay you another day and give me 3 of those nice fresh buns now?" The young man looked up much amused but said nothing, only advanced towards the buns. Mim said, "It was just really very nice of him to do it, that she did thank him

<u>very</u>, and it wasn't frightened he need be, she would be forgetting."

The young man smiled and said "he was sure of it". So Mim took the buns! On second thoughts, she remembered she had a letter in her pocket, and returning to the young man said "I am staying at 'Aldersyde', there is my address if you want to come over!" but she went off triumphing, pointing out to her bairns the advantage of her simple, trustworthy countenance!!

They went by the shore to the best ascent to Peak. Streams of water in every direction forcing their way through the shaley cliffs and spouting out with much force, bringing down much of the shale and evidently causing many a landslip.

Waded through streams and skipped over stepping stones, dried ourselves walking in the sun. Climbed the acclivity, very steep too in places, got up on to the heather, which was quite delicious and had a grand walk entirely.

Mim found the remains of an old hen. Elsie had been complaining of great hunger - Mim offered her the "chicken" to appease it.

Elsie, "It will be tender enough".

Mim, "And tasty too!"

Elsie, "Well flavoured in anycase"

Mim, "High flavoured rather".

Elsie, "At all events, I'll share it with you, Mimsie".

Mim, "I couldn't possibly be so selfish, knowing you so hungry!"

Elsie, "It would be equally selfish for me to enjoy it alone."

Mim, "Sister might like to assist you."

Elsie, "Then I'll take the wing - Sis may enjoy the head - brains and maggots!"

So, we whiled away our long walk! We are often so funny (in our own eyes, but whose else's are there to consider!!!)

Came back also by the shore, the tide being quite sufficiently out still to allow this. Didn't get in till past 6. Mim rather tired. The damp weather makes her a bit inclined to throat. Read "Catriona" after tea. Elsie snuffling violently is accused of a cold by Mim which Elsie violently resents.

Mab says, "Just listen to Elsie how her nose is stuffed!"

Elsie; "I don't see what it matters to you, in what condition I choose to keep my nose."

Mab; "It matters a good deal to me as I have to sleep in your room and I'm not partial to lie listening to your violent and vulgar snufflings, violently vulgar I may call them."

Elsie proceeds to give us an example of her powers in that direction to oblige Mabsie, but Mim interferes and shortly after packed them off to bed, where, let us hope, that violence and sniffing vulgarity and tiffing, will soon be buried in profoundest of slumber, not to be disturbed, either by crashings of thunder, or the powers of Elsie's nose!!

A landslip on the line this afternoon which greatly delayed the evening train from Scarborough. It is no wonder at all after the very violent rains there have been and the nature of the soil here being taken into consideration.

Cliff edge cottages from the shore.

<u>Sunday July 28th</u>

Dull morning, bright intervals but looking threatening more or less all day. Went to church in morning. Mr Cooper is "piano-forte" in his style of elocution as ever. After luncheon went for a walk on the cliffs, met the man on his pony, who, as we believe, assisted to have us warned off the field as trespassers lately. The Girshas comment freely and said "Amen"! All still feeling severe, as they remember the rebuff!! Didn't dare go far as the clouds were so heavy and black and we in our Robin Hood's Bay Sunday Best.

We watched the sand-martens and a few sea gulls, conversed with one of the railway porters who we met out with a beautiful Skye terrier with long hair and the shortest legs imaginable, and heard from him that poison had been put about among the garbage to kill cats who had been trespassing on the cliffs among the rabbits. We told him about Keinz illness and he said many dogs had suffered from this cause and eating the filth. We talked about the little town and the pride everyone has in keeping their houses so smart and clean and he told us that the great matter was that it was all the week long houses were kept so clean and the narrow streets not, a great clean up on Saturdays only.

Mim didn't feel especially bright and is throating, so came in about 4 sending the bairns for a walk with Spittles - they went to the old churchyard.

After tea we read alternately "To right the wrong" by Edna Lyall. On the cliffs in the afternoon we met and Mim recognised the young man who had trusted her about the buns and gave him a confiding nod - she was rather pleased he should see her in her Sunday frock, so that it might inspire him with *additional* confidence in her - tho' she does not fail to impress on the Bairns that her speaking countenance was quite sufficient!! The Girshas grin, say "O Mimsie" but do not respond with the loud acclamation of assent Mim had expected. The baking young man is very fair, rather like Lord Morpeth and wears spectacles.

In the evening Mim played hymns on the piano and other sacred music she could discover here. Elsie drew her this nice little chick which she said "is so like you Mim".

So "like" did she consider it, that having copied it out of Mrs Russell's "Church Monthly", she found it incumbent upon herself to write "Mim" beneath the original in Mrs Russell's book which Mim considered superfluous of her, so will also probably Mrs Russell when next it meets her eye.

We read the Evening Service together and then went to bed - Mim also, as she hasn't been sleeping well and felt a good long lie would probably be beneficial. Rather finer night, at least the thunder restrained itself to mutterings in the afternoon.

St. Stephen's Church.

<u>Monday July 29th</u>

    Fairer, though it is still overclouded, the sun breaking out vividly at odd times. Mr Richardson appeared about 11 and took us to see Sir Charles Strickland's house here. It is the old Manor House and is quite nice, with charming wooden latches to all the doors, which therefore make no noise at all. Mim breaks the 10th Commandment and "covets" violently thinking of the clicking noisy locks at Wigganthorpe. Leaving Mr Richardson we wandered down to the post, Mim intent on paying the young baker.

The old Manor House - now the Methodist Church on Wesley Road.

This successfully accomplished by the bestowal of 3 pence, she further dignified her gratification at his late conduct by spending twopence more in a new roll, which was put in a bag for future use, and one penny on two sticks of liquorice objects much coveted by Mab and Elsie. Sixpence poorer we emerged into the street again and meeting the Captain of the Coast Guard Mim stopped for a long discourse about this place - the fame of the Brig "Romulus" which was lost here on Nov 18th 1893; were anxious to get a young sea gull but the Captain says short of Filey this is impossible, as the nature of the cliffs here makes climbing impossible.

The wreck of the 'Romulus' which came aground with its bowsprit through the windows of the Bay Hotel. Until recently, its figurehead could be seen on the front of York House in King Street.

Paid Monsieur Russell, the grocer and post master a visit - bought postcards, two lemons and ordered some honey. Paid a visit to the photographers. "Are you going to give him a few more lessons Mim and tell him what he ought to do?" says Mab. "Certainly, my pet, and much to his advantage I should do so" says Mim.

Mr Walmsley out - sorra! but Madame slightly *en deshabille* [untidy] appeared and having evidently been warned by Monsieur what to do instinctly, produced prints of the special views Mim had pointed out - both really very good, one especially and copies may be seen next page (turn over!)

Time to get back for dinner is at 12.30 as we have settled to trust our lives to the tender mercies of Mr Goodchild's conveyance and horse and go to see Falling Foss they say some 4½ miles from here but right away over the moors.

There is a charming vagueness about everything to do with Robin Hood's Bay, an atmosphere in which Mim feels very much at home. You are asked to say what you would like

King's Beck from the Bridge, looking upstream.

King's Beck from the Bridge, looking downstream, showing Beck Cottage and the Wesleyan Chapel.

for dinner for example, and whatever you choose, the one answer awaits you, "Yes it will do nicely if we can get it" and that proves a problem, for most times, they can't and you are quite content and think it perfectly natural to find something before you of which you never even wildly dreamt. One day Mim ordered chickens and rice pudding - our dinner, when we sat down to it was cow and mutton chops and a fruit tart but the most vivid imagination would never dream in questioning why!!

    Well, on our way home from the photographers we met Mr Goodchild looking for us and the following conversation ensued.

Mr G. "I was looking for you, my lady, to tell you that the trap will be there at one for you but I thought I had better tell you the boy does not know the way."

Mim (laughing). "Am I to drive it for him, Mr Goodchild? I'll try my best, but I haven't an idea where the Foss lies."

G.(also laughing). "That's why I met you to explain how to go and the boy thinks he knows half way" - followed directions which Mim endeavours inwardly to digest and which she carefully repeats to Mr G. who applauds her retentive memory.

Mim. "But you will tell the boy too, in case I mistake."

Mr G. "Yes, my lady. I have done so and given him a little map of the road."

Mim. "All right then, Mr Goodchild. Goodbye, if we never meet again and you'll promise that if we don't turn up you'll come and look for our remains?"

Mr G. (laughing) "I'll promise you that, my lady, but I think the boy will get all right, with you to help him."

'Charley', Mr. Goodchild's horse.

So we parted - had luncheon, at appointed time appears a cranky looking dog cart, a still crankier looking black horse, who, as Elsie says, "Looks more like a pointer than a horse from the way it carries its head." And instead of Goodchild's "boy" a smart looking young man, got up regardless of expense (and weather) in his quite best and handsomely brushed clothes. Mim mounts alongside of him, Girshas behind - cloaks etc been all stowed in, and we start - or try to! At first, Charley, the horse, refuses to move. A little drawing at the reins from the young man and a little reminding of the whip at last get him to move at a foot's pace.

"No fear of his running away at least" comments Mim. The young man bravely assents to her remark. Meet Goodchild driving a diminutive pony and cart in which he has given a lift to the postman and a child. Something wrong with our harness. Goodchild leaves his trap and settles us up - we start again!! How describe our drive? As Mab says "I hope Mim will not want to take us another drive here, this one is so unique that I would like to preserve it alone in my memory."

We discover that our driver is the butcher "P.N.Beedle" who since the day of arrival, when Mim passed his shop and saw the name she has called "Mr Pin and Needle Butcher" rather to the indignation of the Girshas.

This alone was great fun, next it turned out that he had never, never driven Charley before, nor any other horse either we fancied from his style of driving - the only reason of his coming was his excuse he "knew the road"!!

We did get to the Foss, and we saw it, clambering down at the risk of our lives thro' the slipperiest of mud and the steepest of banks to the rushingest Foss - on the whole worth seeing, but we found disappointing, rather may be from dull day and colouring in consequence - but why we ever got there, ask me not!

Charley preferred any bye road or direction opposite to our destination rather than the way he should go. Mr Pin and Needle tried sawing - failure; whip - failure; a smack right and left - no result; then he rose in his seat and came down with a mighty crash on Charley's back, who then moved on, tho'

The river near Falling Foss.

sometimes with a preference for the ditch. There, too, in places the road was kept together with wooden beams placed across it, rising a little above the loose gravel.

These were Charley's aversion, at those he stopped dead short but Pin and Needle crashed on his back and Charley ambled over, needless to say Mim and the Girshas walked conscientiously up all hills and inclines and down all hills and inclines or very surely it's at Falling Foss or out on the moors we'd be at this moment. We asked the distance this morning. "Four and a half miles." "How long will you be wanting to do it in?" "Four hours, my lady."

Then we started. Now we are sadder and wiser. It came on to rain as we left the Foss, a wetting drizzle, but we have our cloaks with us and Pin and Needle had his overcoat and a waterproof rug.

We all laughed and talked and were very cheery, our conversation duly accompanied by the smacks on Charley's unheeding carcase, but which fell with praiseworthy regularity all the same.

The bairns devoured the bun bought this morning, for their hunger is continuous and they are equally ready for their tea which is ready soon after our return. While changing their damp things Mab and Elsie rehearse this afternoon's adventures, using the bed or empty air as Charley and in turn acting the role of 'Pin and Needle'. Certainly it was a very amusing afternoon, though I don't believe any of us are greatly solicitous to repeat the experiment, nor very highly to recommend Mr Goodchild's apparatus for sight seeing.

Found pleasant letters on return, wrote some - had fire lighted as the evening is distinctly damp - read "Catriona" having finished "Marmion" this morning - discussed our day's adventures and the Girshas trotted off to bed and Mim follows gleefully now she has written up the log.

Good accounts of Keinz though he is still very weak.

Falling Foss.

Tuesday July 30th

Most lovely morning - settled to have a long afternoon on the moors above Peak. Dinner at 12.30 and as soon after as we could collect ourselves and letters and goods and chattels, we embarked for the heather.

Stopped at Moorsom's shop to buy a net bag for carrying sketching materials and provender for hungry bairns. Stopped at Mrs Granger's to buy photograph of Falling Foss. Stopped at our friend the Baker to try and buy some buns. The super excellencies were not fresh to-day so purchased some piping hot scones, very yellow and full of plums and secured in a paper bag. Esconced them in our sack, then along the beach to the second beck [Stoup Beck] and crossing it, this time on stepping stones for the "roaring torrent" was no longer "deep and wide" we clambered up the weary hill to above the railway.

We were all very lazy. The bairns sucked a good deal of liquorice which they cut off in small fragments with a very dirty pocket knife - Mim assisted in the disappearance of the black sponge, for Rob Roy liquorice is remarkably soft. Then we struggled on again - very certainly we were morally limp if not physically, however, having at last attained the heather we greatly revived. At 4.30 we produced our scones and had our little meal - the bairns falling also upon the bilberries which they ate till their mouths inside and out were dyed the deepest purple and Mim made them wash themselves in her painting water, for she was feebly struggling with an ugly sketch in which multitudinous fragments still decked the Moors. Mab found some white heather and we carefully dug out the plant and sent it later off to Wigganthorpe in hopes it will grow.

Tide very much out today and we walked back that way, looking for curiosities. Elsie had found a nice piece of pumice stone and we all discovered ammonites more or less imperfect, dug them out and brought them back.

We didn't get to 'Aldersyde' till past 6 when a little tea was by no means unwelcome. Nothing wildly exciting transpired between us today.

We went on with "Catriona" but the girls went early to bed. Mim read "Venetian Life" and "A Child of the Age" over the fire till she went to sleep - when she awoke, she also went to bed!

Robin Hood's Bay looking north from the foot of the cliffs at Ravenscar.

<u>Wednesday July 31st</u>

A much better account of my Keinzerli this morning - "improving, able to take a little exercise and a little solid food." Mim greatly revived after the post therefore.

A dull overcast day, everything looking the same colour out of doors, sea, sky, land, everything. Read "Plutarch's Lives" and "Sans Famille" for lessons.

Then the Girshas went out with Spittles, leaving Mim to draw and write her letters before luncheon. She was good enough to give the bairns a second dose of the French after that *repas copieux* [hearty meal] was faithfully accomplished by them, bless them and their dear little ever ready tummies!!! -

Then we went out - No gigantic project in view, thinner shoes and calmer points of view, longer skirts and milder ambitions, smarter hats and a general air of higher respectability pervaded them somehow this afternoon. To the station for stamps and to the town, then the cliffs, then to first beck then back by the shore. Needless to say we stopped Mr Durrant the baker and bought buns for our walk - likewise buns for tea and a brown loaf, likewise Ann pastelles in a bag. The young spectacled man smiles mysteriously when he sees us advancing. Mim is very forward with her purse, even if, for the moment said purse is only an old envelope, she is so anxious he should see she does not always mean to encroach on his trustfulness. Still he persists in that mysterious smile.

No further adventures to relate nor did we find any treasures of note on the beach, tho' we sighted a jelly fish and had ideas of carrying it out to sea but the tide was very low and the jelly fish very arduous to carry and we didn't.

The Girshas skirmished upstairs with a noise of thunder produced by their fairy feet at sight of a baby in the kitchen, which Mim went to inspect - and which proved to be a niece of Mrs Russell's. After tea we read "Catriona" - has amused us much, and which draws very closely to its end, sorra!

We read alternately and pursue our usual and various hard occupations the while. We realize how soon our time here is over. Mim, the most sentimental, is sorry that the nice little quiet life here is so soon to end, says "it is always the case when a time is over that one feels regret." The bairns say "does one?" but there are ponies and kittens at Wigganthorpe!!!

Mim keeps her reflections to herself and subsides!

Thursday August 1st

Good accounts of Keinz. Got up betimes so as to start by 9.26 train for Runswick Bay. Fine morning inclined to feel thundery. A letter from Mr Charles Bourke tells me that Keith Fraser died suddenly on board the "Mirage" while cruising with O. I am dreadfully sorry - no other detail given and the York Herald does not mention it. London papers arrive later. Met Captain of Coast Guard at the station, invited us to go and see Rocket apparatus etc. tomorrow which we are delighted to do.

Interesting line to Runswick, many curious bits of the coast, Sandsend, Kettleness and ultimately Runswick itself, a most romantic spot, only a fishing village, no house much bigger than a cottage, and these cottages scattered up the cliff anyhow, no two facing the same way and as at Robin Hood's Bay, eminently picturesque with their bright scarlet roofs and the mist of smoke from all the little chimnies which seem perpetually to pervade them and gives the place a dreamy, half unreal look.

Picturesque cottages at Runswick Bay.

Hinderwell was the station for Runswick, arrived there we got out and followed the little train of other tourists through some fields on to a remarkably dull road which led past the little hotel to the top of the cliff from which we looked down on the tops of little red roofed houses scrambling down the steep cliff, one on top of the other to the sea, far below, looking very sparkling and blue under today's bright sky. On our way to the cliff we passed houses evidently occupied by artists one or two who appeared with the inevitable wild hair, slouched hats etc of their "trade" as Mab called it and Mim remonstrated her veneration for Art feeling itself inquired thereby.

All the same, to the question why? these peculiarities of *neglige* and costume are necessary, Mim has no answer to give. "Not knowing can't say my dear, unless it is a feeling for the picturesque." Mab sees no picturesqueness in looking frightful. There's something in that too!! We went down to the shore, every step delighting us, the quaintness defies description.

The village seems built on a series of very narrow terraces made just as came convenient, or, probably, as the ground lent itself, the delightful irregularity being impossible on any other assumption. Narrowest of little stone lanes, either paved with flags, or with round uneven pebbles and everlasting steps connecting houses and terraces. These we follow as they lead you, coming suddenly on a bit of bright garden or a small court hung with all the needfuls of the fishing trade, coils of brown ropes, nets, corked ropes, bales, coloured bladders of the brightest greens, blues, oranges, hanging in festoons, a picture everywhere but how impossible to sketch in so limited a time, one small attempt being all Mim could achieve.

The bairns had provided themselves with unappetising looking sandwiches which they prepare to assimilate but against which Mim's soul revolted. So as there was nothing else and she had forgotten to take anything with her and only a cup of coffee at 8 she thought she would wander up to the village and see what the nakedness of the land would be producing.

Arriving at the "Grocery" asked for bread, was told they kept none but I would find all I wanted at Prospect House, the Refreshment Rooms, went there, was told they were always delighted to supply strangers whenever they had anything, but at the present they had nothing - laughed and enquired was there a baker anywhere. Yes, and directions to find him given.

Found out the bake house - locked, however, roaming about saw a man in the neighbourhood looking somewhat flour-ey. Asked him was he the baker? Said he was hard of hearing. Roared the question again, smiling sweetly at him as apology for bawling. Said he was, asked if he would give me some bread? He agreed.

Back we went to the bake house and I got the needments - purchased also a portion of cheese, knowing the Girshas weakness in that direction. Returned heavily laden to the beach and proceeded to feed my young, an attenuated hound, and a herd of famished fowl, was all collected round me.

We found it all very good - and the remains we bestowed on various infants haunting the strand with wooden spades and scarlet pails, and boys who apparently considered the heads of antique Cod, playthings after their heart - one little toddler was so impressed with the excellency of rice cake that he totally forgot his red pail and wandered off munching and blessed, and full of oblivion as well as provender.

Our meal finished, we went to explore and curious it most certainly was and only like itself.

Ultimately found our way back to the station - partook there of bad ginger beer, watched the hives of bees, and the Station Master's ducks and hens and waited our 1.36 train to Whitby.

Then we watched them unloading the herrings, carrying them off in barrels, 12 dozen in each to the shore, where they were poured into bigger barrells, at all events, barrells packed to the brim nicely, room only being left for a layer of ice, then a piece of paper over the ice, then straw tied over all. It was interesting to watch and everything so quickly done.

We had a little tea at our old friend, the confectioners and got to the station in time for the 4.21 train and so back here, very glad to get in but feeling we had had a very nice day. We finished "Catriona" and began "The Haven under the Hill" in the evening.

Amongst the tourists at Runswick was a very characteristic English papa, likewise a Mama with a bonnet and brown parasol - two daughters in light blue shirts and dark skirts and Mim felt convinced, a cousin in mustardy brown.

One sprightly Miss, Mim named the Alpin climber, she invariably walked on the tips of her toes and displayed a tendency for seeking dangerous places to climb. Papa remonstrated - "My dear girl, I advise you not to try that. Look at me, I've never imperilled my life yet and I don't mean to do so now."

Mab and I agreed we were very assured he said no more than the truth, it needed only to follow his injunction and "look". The Alpin Climber refrained therefore from her wild intentions, but proceeded to rush up the road with frantic endeavour - Fat cousin followed, at first with spirit, but the nature of things forbade a long continuance of her ardour and she stopped, panting and puffing and no doubt perspiring at every pore, for it was exceptionally hot and close.

The cousin likewise wore spectacles. The other daughter assumed a *degage [easy, casual]* and masculine air, swung her stick round and round, walked with big, rather rolling steps, by no means undesirous of attracting notice. Papa fussing about and full of conversation and explanation. Mama placid, and somewhat stately in her dress, rather tight about the waist which Mim fancied incommoded her on the steeply upward way! but who knows?

They got into our train but after Hinderwell platform, we saw them no more, as far as we are concerned they disappeared and left not a trace behind except a memory in our minds.

Marvellous arrangements as to tickets, only conceivable to the Whitby mind, but we agree to everything without demur, feeling it soars above our poor comprehension, far -.

Walked through the town on to the pier, watched herring boats come in, looking so nice with their dark brown sails and making the harbour so neatly with a favourable wind.

Fishing boats in Whitby harbour.

Friday August 2nd

Our last day here. Mim is sorry. Bairns full of beans and packing, much rustling is heard about stairs and bedroom, rustlings of packing papers, opening of cupboards and drawers, creaking of box lids etc.

However, when the inexorable Mim comes down, she by no means considers leaving tomorrow and read on why "Sans Famille" should not be continued to-day! and we do our French, and finish the Life of Themistoche conscientiously. After this, the Girshas departed for a walk. Mim writes her letters.

Luncheon, then Mim takes the packing craze and our poor sitting room soon looks bare - book box packed and closed - the few adornments we have consigned to their respective trunks and a general air of "waiting for the train" has succeeded to the very comfey appearance we presented for the last 3 weeks.

The Revd. Jermyn Cooper called on us yesterday, so to-day we went to call on him - saw his charming garden, were

In the Vicarage Garden.

introduced to his 3 "Misses" and asked to have tea. Mim accepted, if we might return for we were engaged between 3 and 4 to the Coast Guard - Agreed - We then went down the hill to the port, met the Captain who took us over the Station, showed us everything connected with the Coast Guard, cutlasses, carbines, stickswords, revolvers, everything. He says that comparatively little smuggling goes on there now, but at times they have severe cases.

Coastguard House and Board of Trade Rocket Apparatus headquarters, the Slipway.

Then helped by two of the men he showed us how the rockets worked, very interesting - had never seen it before - showed us pictures of the way it acted, and everything was done thorough, bar the actual firing even to taking the plug out and putting in the fuse. Each thing too, we examined separately, and the way they acted was fully explained to us and the cost and its fittings displayed. The bairns also looked through the telescope at the Station.

Visited our friend the Baker and made our fond 'adoos' - to the photographer's and ordered the revised photographs!

Then we returned to the Rectory and had tea - everyone there very kind and pleasant. About 6 we returned here, the Rector walking part of the way with us and giving Mim some lovely roses.

Thundering finely in the distance and thunderously black over Peak. Then it rained and after came the most beautiful rainbow and even two reflections which lasted for long, intensely bright in colour. The lights were quite lovely this evening and colour vivid against the threatening darker livid sky. Suddenly the gas burns low - almost out - is Hamlet's Ghost about?!!?

'Peak' Ravenscar from the beach.

<u>Saturday August 3rd</u>

Though no ghost did appear, yet the fluctuations of light and shade prevented the continuing any writing, not that there was much more to say last night.

Elsie is supposed to be "pea green" this morning Mab informed me "that I may look out for Elsie's being sick sometime or other today, for she has been watching her and seen unmistakeable signs and you see Mimmie, my long experience has made me a professor in Elsie's symptoms."

Elsie meanwhile protests that it is only on economical principles she avoids breakfast as contingencies being possible, she sees no use in waste.

Bare, bleak look over our rooms this morning. "Family leaving" plainly inscribed on everything, ourselves included.

Mr Cooper arrived *de grand matins* [early in the morning]. Mim still wallowing in the hot bath and brought her a lovely bouquet of roses. Mim could hardly ask him to enter! Partly later than meant to be, as she was pre-occupied making "green pea" soap bales for the Pelse.

Keinz very improving, is today's news of my beautiful Brown.

Mab and Mimmie walked to Rectory to thank for bouquet, only the "Misses" in.

Then we went to Mr Peter Moorsom's an old fisherman, whose 82 birthday it was and Mim gave him a comforter she had made for him for pleasure. Then to Mrs Granger's Fancy Repository where Mab bought a cup and saucer with Robin Hood's Bay on it, a commission for Spittles.

Next to fat Mr Moorsom's the grocer etc who had charge of Mab's shrimp net which wanted mending. Mim asked him "did she owe him anything"? Mr Moorsom wasn't aware that she did - but that is a trifle here, whatever you do or not. Nobody seems to mind. They are perfectly willing to forget and go without. It was only by the most persistent honesty that Mim compelled the baker to take a certain 6d she owed him for 6 memorable buns of his of such an excellent nature that their yellow ghosts still haunt our remembrances. He had forgotten he said!

Meanwhile, this being our last visit to the portly and spectacled Moorsom, Mim told Mabsie she would de-prive herself of the pleasure of kissing the dear man Good-bye herself, in order that Mab might have it instead. She begs Mab will note and admire her Mimsie's beautiful unselfish disposition.

Strange to say it didn't seem to strike Mab in that light, the young and foolish should be grateful Mim thinks and discants on the situation, but Mab only laughs!

At luncheon Mim proposes to make an offer to Mr Goodchild for "Charley" the "pointer" who took us, or rather accompanied us to the Foss. Mab and Elsie stare indignant. "Buy him and send him to the kennels" says Elsie. "He'll do for Keinz to eat" says Mab. "Charley soup for Keinz" says Elsie. Soon after luncheon we broke up our camp and started for the Station a pied [on foot], naturally, leaving Spittles to bring up the rear with "Charley", Mr Goodchild and our bales.

Siskin in his red cloth-covered cage. "Blob head - Pinbody" the Canary in his cage covered with brown paper ambled off with us.

We went by the Coast Line this time, passed our happy hunting grounds of former afternoons on the way to Scarborough.

Every train was late, every connection missed, waited consequently several consecutive hours at Scarboro', several more at Malton and only got to Wigganthorpe about 6.30 instead of 4.15.

At Malton conversed Johnson respecting my beautiful Brown, who is much better but was quite desperately ill at one time and Johnson was greatly alarmed.

And so we got back, and our little expedition is ended.

Mab and Elsie are brown and ravenous and on the whole rejoicing in robust health. Mimsie, the old hen feels she need no longer quack plaintively over the "delicate" appearance of her ducklings (and make them furious by the operation)!! but may, while she sits calmly in her henroost, writing the last words of the log, liken them both to fat "Babes of Bashan" (greatly pleasing the ducklings thereby) and cluck complacently, very satisfied with the results of our experiences of Robin Hood's Bay.

4/6